NOW, Not Later

Make More Money
IMMEDIATELY

Bob Poole

First published in 2020 by Liverpool Press
Robert W. Poole
First Edition

ISBN 978-0-9824208-4-3

Library of Congress Control Number:2019918873

Dedication

for Joann

Contents

Preface

I DID SOME SALES AND MARKETING WORK WITH a guy back in the 1980s who was one of the more colorful people I've met in my career. Charismatic, good looking, with a silver tongue, he was one of those people you either like and enjoy right away... or whom you immediately dislike.

I was in the former category. He had one major character flaw, however, that never ceased to cause him trouble: He always thought there was a quicker, easier way to make money.

Easier, for him, fell into the categories of appropriating other people's ideas, copyrighted material, and so on. In his opinion, following "the rules" was something that stood in the way of him getting what he wanted — right now. He was content to let other people play that game, while he was always looking for a way to get rich quick without putting in the work.

While the title of this little book is *Now, Not Later: Make More Money Immediately*, it is not a "get rich quick" recipe book. It is a *formula* — one that, if followed, will allow you to put into action legitimate plans for increasing your income. It is a book about listening to what people tell you they want and need and then learning how to provide it for them. It also teaches you to do this in a way that separates you from the people whose focus is on bending the rules, taking the shortcuts, and refusing to listen.

Let your focus be one of providing value for people — all people — not just ones you are trying to sell. You'll find that doors will open, ideas will germinate and grow, and resources will become available. You'll be able to enjoy the life you visualize and the monetary rewards you deserve... all while you help others get what they want and need.

— Bob Poole
January, 2020

Everybody Wants More Money

I REMEMBER SEEING A CRAIGSLIST AD ONCE FOR somebody's daily ride, a Jeep Cherokee. The person selling the Cherokee was selling it for maybe half of what the vehicle was worth. "Must sell before this weekend," said the ad. "Otherwise I can't pay my rent."

Something about that really bothered me.

The thought of somebody selling their car just to make rent, just to buy time before another, inevitable crisis a month later, kind of burned me. It burned me because there's always money out there. We live in a world that is absolutely *awash* in cash. Now, yes, some of those opportunities require that you already have a little money to take advantage of them. Others don't. The reality, though, is that there are countless ways to make money in the world. The money is just waiting for you to earn it, to make it, and to put it to work for you.

The challenge, though, is that while all the money in the world is just waiting to be earned… too many people don't know how. They *want* the money, sure. They need the money, most definitely. Like that poor person selling their Jeep to make rent, they need cash and are sometimes absolutely desperate for it. They don't need the promise of money. They don't need the opportunity to make money later. They need money *right now*. They don't know how to get it, however, and because they don't know how, they assume they can't.

They're wrong.

Everyone can make more money. Most importantly, though, everyone can make more money *right now*. It's not even a complicated challenge to solve. You just need the tools to go out there and earn what you need from the world. But, no, let me correct that. You don't just need the tools. In some cases, you may also need to learn — and even to unlearn — a few things about money. Your attitude about money, and about work, might need to change a little.

I know mine did.

When I learned to have the right attitude about money, I never had to worry about getting enough again.

Neither will you.

Let's start, though, with the three reasons you aren't making enough money. A couple of these probably seem like common sense. One of them might surprise you. All three, however, matter.

THE 3 REASONS YOU AREN'T MAKING ENOUGH MONEY

There are any number of reasons you aren't making money. Some of these things might be out of your control. An illness that makes it difficult for you to work, the loss of a job in which you had a lot of time and experience invested... these things can make it difficult for you. They aren't something you can't overcome, but they're temporary. They have obvious explanations.

When I talk about the three reasons you aren't making enough money, I'm talking about systemic challenges — life challenges, in other words. I'm talking about things that might even have been holding you back for your whole life. The specifics are different from person to person, but there's basically just three reasons: You aren't working enough, you aren't working smart enough, or you aren't working to provide enough value.

You Aren't Working ENOUGH

The simplest reason, and the easiest thing to correct, is the challenge of not working enough. Most of us don't live to work. We work to live — to get what we need to get by. We work to put food on the table, pay our other bills, provide for our families, maybe have a little left over on the side.

Very few of us are driven to amass vast wealth (although we'd all take it if it were offered to us). We know that we could make twice as much money working 80 hours a week, but most of us don't take that path. The overwhelming majority of people who work simply work a single 40-hour-per-week job, and they get by on what they make.

Does that describe you? Are you working just one job trading time for money? At the end of the year, do you file a single 1040EZ with one source of income and maybe a little interest income from a bank account? That describes a lot more people than you might think. In some ways, that's the American dream — working your job and having the rest of your time to yourself. Most of us can't imagine working more than that.

The challenge is, when you work just one job and then clock out and go home, you're never earning any MORE money. You have what you have... and nothing more. If you come up against a sudden or unexpected expense, from a medical bill to a car repair to a fancy television you want to buy, you have two choices. You can go without, or you can put the bill on a credit card.

If you do the latter, like so many people, you end up with credit card bills that take forever to pay off. Add in the interest that you'll pay on those credit cards and you're paying a LOT of money over time. If you had more income, you'd be able to pay off those bills. You'd also have extra cash for the unexpected and even to put some away. A staggering amount of people have no savings, or almost no savings. Does this describe you?

The simple solution is to work more. The "gig economy" is a good example of the growing number of people who have figured this out. More and more people are taking on "side hustles." These are side jobs they do to make extra money.

They're trading their time and money to make extra money over and above their "day jobs." Some of them are even using those "gig" jobs, those side hustles, to make ALL their income, scaling the number of hours they work to match what they want to make. They drive for Uber or Lyft, or they sell crafts on Etsy, or they take part time jobs, or they participate in virtual freelance marketplaces like Upwork. Heck, some people are making their car payments and then some just buying stuff from thrift stores and selling it on eBay.

What they all have in common is that they are working MORE. If you're not making enough money, one way to start making more money RIGHT NOW is to work more. This is simply a matter of identifying how you want to earn and then earning, right? Well, no; there's a little more to it than that. But we'll get to that.

You Aren't Working SMART ENOUGH

The second reason people aren't making enough money is that they're not working "smart" enough. These are people who are putting in a lot of hours... but they're simply not making enough income despite all the work they do. Do you know people like that? They always seem to be working... but they never seem to be getting ahead. They're always busy... but they don't seem to have any more cash than they did before they took on all that extra work. What are they doing wrong?

Working smart means running the numbers to see if what you are doing is actually profitable. For example, if you drive for Uber, but your car expenses are essentially erasing your extra income (especially if the price of gas is rising), you'd be better off finding something else to do (or staying home). If you work a part-time job, but it costs you a huge chunk of your earnings to pay for day care while you're at that part-time job, it makes no sense to do that work.

Likewise, you may have a decent side income... but you might be underpaid. Maybe you undervalued yourself when you took the job, or maybe you started out in the market at a low rate and your pay increases over the years haven't caught up with the prevailing wage for that job. Undervaluing yourself is a huge reason why you aren't making enough money. It could be that leaving a comfortable, familiar job that pays you too little, and going to a new job where they are willing to pay you what you are worth, is in order.

There are plenty of other ways to work smarter, not harder. If you aren't working smart enough, you'll never get ahead, even if you are working crazy "overtime" hours. Our goal is not to work you to death. The goal of this book is to teach you how to make more money, right now, in a way that actually benefits you. That means making sure that whatever job you do is profitable. The numbers have to add up... or it's time to do something else.

You Aren't Working To PROVIDE ENOUGH VALUE

The last category, the last reason, is the most complicated one. The reason you might not be making enough money could be because, despite all the work you're doing, you're simply not providing enough value. This could be value provided to an employer, or it could be value provided to a marketplace.

Providing value means that you do something that people are willing to pay you for, and that not just anyone can do. Do you remember the scene from the film "Office Space," in which the two job auditors are interviewing an employee who essentially does nothing? He gets very irate when the auditors suggest that there's no real reason for what he does — that he adds no real value to the process. "I'm a *people* person!" he insists. Meanwhile, it's clear to the audience that he's going to get laid off, because he doesn't add value.

If you're currently being paid a low wage and it's because you don't add enough value, don't worry. There are lots of ways you can start adding more value. This will sometimes require creativity on your part. It will almost always involve hard work.

And sometimes, it will mean you have to change what you're doing completely because what you're doing now just doesn't offer enough opportunity. We're going to provide you with lots of ideas for how you can supplement your income in the course of this book... and these will allow you either to pad your income while you're making lower wages, or leave that lower wage job behind completely. You may even find that the ideas this book provides will help you unlock a new mindset — one that will help you make positive changes in your work life as you move forward. For now, the least you need to know is that, if you're not making enough money, there is always a way to get more... even if it means embarking on some projects you never before considered.

YOU NEED PRACTICAL SOLUTIONS FOR MAKING MORE MONEY NOW

Like that poor Craigslist advertiser, you don't need inspirational slogans. You don't need the equivalent of a poster showing a kitten hanging from a branch that says, "Hang in there!" You need practical solutions to the challenge of not making enough money. More importantly, you need to start making MORE money right NOW. The good news is, this book is going to teach you to do that.

Where Do We Go From Here?

We're going to start by explaining to you why you need to sell. You may not realize it now, but a big part of making more money is learning to sell — sell products, sell services, and even sell yourself. We'll address the reasons you think you can't sell, and we'll teach you how to overcome those issues.

Next, we'll delve into the practical nuts and bolts of selling. We'll teach you how to evaluate what you should be selling, run the math to make sure the numbers add up, and even teach you some basic strategies for thinking "outside the box" to adapt your money-making concept.

We won't just leave you with strategies, though. We'll also teach you HOW to sell. We'll explain the principles behind the process of selling, and we'll give you a proven system for working it out. By the time we're done, you'll not only be prepared to make more money, but you'll be eager to get out there and start claiming some of that endless supply of money that's waiting to be made.

Finally, we'll leave you with some practical possibilities and examples. You may feel free to take and use these examples as money making opportunities. We think, though, that they're more useful as jumping-off points. They're ideas that you can leverage and apply to your own specific situation in order to make more money in the way that's best for you.

At the end of this book, you'll find a checklist of action steps. These will explain what you need to do to get started... and will leave you with some advice to get you out there.

That's it. It doesn't get any more complicated than that. By the time you're done with this book, you'll be kicking yourself for not thinking of it before. It's actually very simple to make more money. It may involve hard work, and it may require you to put in the time as well as the effort... but then, you knew that. You wouldn't be reading this book if you were afraid of hard work. You just need the tools to get you started making more money... right now.

Are you ready to begin?

Good. Let's get started.

You Need to Sell

NOW, BEFORE YOU GET SCARED, LET ME EXPLAIN. The idea of *selling* bothers some people. It scares them because they believe there's a fundamental challenge to sales. They think it's the person doing the buying who decides, and therefore determines the salesperson's success or failure. It's not. Success or failure in sales is determined by the *seller*.

Let's say you're looking for a job. You find that you can be hired, and easily, at a car dealership. There you learn that the reason they'll hire you so quickly is because your pay is only commission. If you sell many new cars, you'll make a great wage. If you don't sell enough cars, you won't make enough money to pay your bills. This isn't a hypothetical scenario, either. It was a real experience on the part of a friend of mine. He was unemployed and took a job at a dealership... only to find, in his mind, that it was the customers who determined whether he succeeded or failed.

Sales bothers many people, therefore, because they consider it to be "doing something to others." They think it's manipulating other people into buying. It's not either. Real selling is a win-win. You think of sales as trying to *persuade* people to buy, don't you? That concept probably bothers you because you don't like the thought of trying to *make* someone believe you, side with you, or buy what you're selling.

The challenge with that attitude is that... well, it's wrong. Sales isn't about making people do anything. When you sell, you're not putting a gun to someone's face and demanding their money in exchange for your goods or services. That's not sales; that's robbery with some nice parting gifts.

We're going to talk about sales, and selling, in more detail. I can picture what you're thinking right now, though: *I need to make more money, but I'm not interested in chasing commissions.* That's fine. There are jobs where you can work part time for commission, and we may touch on those as we give you ideas for how to make money... but you really don't need to worry about that right now.

This isn't a book about sales *as such*. It's a book about the different ways that you can make money. You need to understand that sales, the act of selling, is a component of absolutely everything in the world of commerce. And, while we're at it, let's make sure we're clear about something else: If you think the "world of commerce" doesn't apply to you, you're wrong.

Every minimum wage worker is engaged in an act of commerce. Every person selling homemade jewelry on Etsy is engaged in an act of commerce. Every Uber driver, every lawyer and accountant, every janitor and restaurant server and librarian and retail shop clerk... they're all engaged in an act of commerce. They're exchanging something they do or something they provide for money.

The thing they provide might be something they made, or it might simply be something they bought and resold. The thing they do could be any act, from assembling components in a factory to driving a bus to housesitting your cat. But every time money (or trade goods) change hands for something you do or something you provide, commerce is happening. *Every act of commerce contains a sales component.*

IT'S ALL ABOUT SELLING

Every idea we're going to share with you in this book, therefore, involves some kind of selling. Some methods of selling are more direct, more obvious, than others. When you sit for a job interview, you're selling. Specifically, you're selling yourself. It doesn't matter if the job itself has nothing to do with sales as such. I don't care if you're interviewing to work behind the counter at Burger King or to become the CEO of a Fortune 500 company. You're still selling yourself to the interviewer.

If you sell goods you made, or resell goods you obtain, regardless of the venue (from eBay to business-to-business sales and even door to door), the sales component is obvious. Simply doing your job well, even where you don't interact with customers, is also an act of sales.

Everybody Sells

There's an old business concept that has found its way, directly or indirectly, into multiple books on sales: Everybody sells. This doesn't just mean that we're all engaged in something that has a sales component, like I've just described. It also means that everyone within a company, no matter what their role, sells to the company's customers.

Say you work for a large company. The business doesn't matter, as long as that business has customers. Every customer who calls or visits your company is given an impression of who you are as a business entity by the people with whom they interact. If every single person they encounter is cheerful, polite, and helpful to them, they'll be much more likely to buy from you — or to buy more — than they would otherwise.

If they encounter a single person with a bad attitude, whether it's the receptionist, a random employee in the hallway, or somebody pushing a broom, it doesn't matter if that's not the person they came to see. Their attitude toward the company will be affected by the experience. In this way, every single person in a company sells to that company's customer base.

Individually, we all sell, even where there is no commerce. Your interactions with the people around you are all about sales. Most of the time, you're selling the commodity that is you. You're selling the people in your world on the benefits of keeping you around. If you are helpful, cheerful, caring, and responsible, you make friends and people like to spend time with you.

If, on the other hand, you're constantly a drag to be around, even your own family members will start to distance themselves. You're selling them, not on the benefits of having you around, but on the benefits of being anywhere that you're not. The same is true even in spousal relationships. You're always "selling" your spouse on the benefits of the marriage. Neglect this and you'll start to watch your marriage crumble.

We're not going to get too deeply into things that don't have making more money in mind. We can't ignore, however, that sales is part of everything we do and everything we are. But if selling is so important, why do so many people hate and fear it?

Why do they think of it the way they think of public speaking? Survey after survey shows that people fear talking in front of others to be an utterly terrifying idea. They're not too much more excited about the idea of selling to their fellow human beings. Why is that?

WHY YOU AREN'T SELLING

There are reasons you think you can't sell. You may not even think of it in those terms. The idea can turn into a chicken-and-egg scenario fairly quickly. You don't sell because you haven't been successful in selling. You haven't been successful because you don't try to sell. The vicious cycle perpetuates itself and the idea of "sales" becomes truly terrifying to contemplate. Boil it all down, though, and there are really only three reasons you aren't selling...which means there are really only three reasons you aren't making more money RIGHT NOW.

You're Afraid to Sell

This is the most obvious one. You aren't selling because you're afraid to sell. Trying to "get other people to buy" is truly terrifying to some of us. I've talked to people who seem to believe you're born with a "sales gene." Either you magically possess the ability to sell, or you have to find and hire someone who does, right? Wrong. Anyone can sell... but, just as fear of public speaking makes it very difficult for some of us to talk in front of crowds, fear of selling makes it very hard for some people to make money.

You Don't Know HOW to Sell

Let's say you aren't scared of the idea of selling, but you have no idea how to go about it. Maybe your attempts to sell in the past were all eager and well-intentioned, but you still failed. Well, there's a good chance you failed because you were doing it wrong. There are a few generally accepted "right ways" to sell... and an almost infinite supply of wrong ones. If you don't know how to approach sales then, no, you won't make money.

You Don't Know WHAT to Sell

The third reason you aren't selling may simply be that you don't know what to sell. Maybe you have all the courage in the world, and maybe you've either learned, or were born with a natural inclination toward, selling. All that talent and willingness won't help if you don't know how to use them to earn. For example, you may be a great salesman, but without a product to sell, you won't get very far. On the other hand, you may have great instincts when it comes to selling, but you may not understand that YOU are the "good or service" being sold in some situations (such as job interviews). If you don't know what to sell and when to sell it, you won't make money.

DON'T WORRY; THIS BOOK CAN HELP

The good news is that this book will teach you how to meet and overcome those challenges. If you're afraid of selling, don't worry; we're going to teach you now to eliminate fear. If you don't know how to sell, that's not a issue; we're going to give you a blueprint for how to approach sales. If you don't know what you should sell, or the best times for doing it, that's okay; we're going to explain to you how to determine that. Everything you need to start making more money right away can be found on these pages.

If this sounds complicated to you, please don't be nervous. It's not that hard. We're going to break down everything so that it's easy to understand. By the time you're done reading this book, you'll know exactly what to do to get started earning. Well, no, that's not entirely accurate. You'll know exactly what to do in order to *figure out* exactly what to do. Everyone's situation is different. Everyone has different abilities and resources. The concepts you must apply to your situation and your resources, however, are universal. They're the foundation of selling. They're the building blocks of making more money *immediately*.

Ready to start getting into the nuts and bolts? Great. Keep reading.

Overcoming the
Fear of Selling

MOST PEOPLE DON'T SELL — DIRECTLY OR INDI-
rectly, in a sales capacity or as part of marketing their goods and
services — because they're afraid. This is perfectly understandable.
Fear is what most often holds us back no matter what we're
talking about. It's a valuable emotion because it prevents us
from doing stupid, reckless things that could make us worse
off. The challenge is, if we don't learn to overcome fear when
it's necessary to grow, we will forever be stuck where we now
find ourselves.

In other words, it's a good thing to be afraid of standing at
the edge of a cliff. That fear prevents you from falling off and
falling to your death. It's a bad thing, however, to be so afraid of

selling that you never start earning money that could otherwise be yours. You won't expand a business, grow as an entrepreneur, or pay your bills through a stable sideline income if you're so afraid of the selling component that you never move forward with your plan.

Overcoming fear isn't always easy... but it doesn't have to be impossibly hard, either. The way you'll overcome the fears you have depends on the source of those fears. If we target those sources and apply strategies for overcoming them, we can get past our fear and start making money *right now*.

FEAR OF PUBLIC SPEAKING

Selling to other people, whether it's selling yourself, selling a product, selling a service, or some other component of sales (and therefore of making more money right now), usually means talking to people. It might be entirely online and in e-mail, or otherwise in writing... but in many cases, it's going to involve communicating in person. In other words, it falls under the heading of public speaking. The thing is, many people are *utterly terrified* of public speaking.

In fact, multiple surveys[1] show that people fear public speaking more than they fear death. That's not as absurd as it sounds. None of us (well, I guess with few notable exceptions) has any experience dying. Every single one of us, however, has had to speak, or at least thought about speaking, to other people. In many cases we are intimidated by that. We don't like people looking at us, waiting to hear from us, and possibly criticizing what we have to say. We don't want to look foolish. We don't want to stammer and struggle for the words. We don't want to be humiliated.

These are the reasons you fear public speaking, aren't they? They all seem like perfectly reasonable fears, too. The thing is, you don't have to be afraid of public speaking. Fear of public speaking can be overcome. It doesn't take any fancy tricks or techniques. All it takes is practice — and a one- or two-time dose of courage.

---

1   https://www.psychologytoday.com/us/blog/the-real-story-risk/201211/the-thing-we-fear-more-death

I'll explain. A friend of mine, who is both a writer and a podcast host (as he likes to say, you can swing your arms in an empty room and hit three or four writers who host their own podcasts) once described to me how he got into college radio (and then into podcasting). Most people can't imagine just switching on a microphone and speaking off the top of their heads for an hour or more. Yet, that's exactly what this fellow does. It all started with a public speaking class that was the very first class he ever took in college.

He explained to me that in that first class, on the very first day of college, he sat there silently with the other students awaiting the professor. All that changed when an outgoing female student turned to him and asked him his name. That's it. That single act of courage was enough to start a conversation, break the ice, and get more people talking.

Using that act of courage as a jumping off point, he never again worried about talking to other people. He just started, simply by asking them their names and then telling them his own. People are remarkably disarmed when they know your name — and when they realize you care about theirs. That single act of courage to speak publicly doesn't have to be asking someone their name, though. It can be anything: Walking up to a crowd of people and asking them a survey question, telling a joke to people you don't know, joining in a conversation in public that's already going on (as long as you do it politely), etc.

What supports that act of courage is practice. By this I mean that you must practice what you want to say — your sales pitch. Don't memorize a speech. Tell a story. When you tell a story that you already know, something that illustrates your point, you don't have to worry about memorizing lines. You just have to explain what you already know. You'll be more comfortable and the people you talk to will be more comfortable. The more you practice your story, which supports your sales pitch, the more easily you will be able to deliver it in the future.

Remember: Start with a single act of courage. Use that to begin telling your story. Practice telling your story over and over again. In no time, your fear of public speaking will be gone, and you'll be comfortable giving your sales pitch.

Compared to fear of public speaking, the other fears are simple and easy to overcome. They all have relatively simple solutions. These include fear of the unknown, fear of financial failure, fear of rejection, fear of overwork, fear of mistakes, fear of conflict, and a number of other specific worries that all have the same solution.

FEAR OF THE UNKNOWN

The first time you do anything you haven't done, you'll be afraid. The unknown bothers us. We are entirely comfortable doing things we've done before. We are often uncomfortable doing new things. The only way to conquer the fear of the unknown is to make that unknown... well, *known*.

I remember a television show called "Top Shot" that involved competitive shooters. The shooters would be exposed to a kind of trial competition, and then they would compete for real a day or two later. In the meantime, they sat around a house full of cameras, talking and producing cut-away videos for use on the reality show. They were divided into two teams, all of them experienced and skilled shooters, archers, and even knife throwers.

In one episode, one team decided to put its down time to good use. Based on the trial competition, they practiced the skills they thought they might face in the very much unknown "real" competition to come. Using mini-golf clubs as stand-ins for their rifles, or just using their hands, they went through the motions of several different competition maneuvers. They couldn't shoot anything; they didn't have guns. But what they could do was train their minds and bodies for the mechanics of the competition. They turned the *unknown* into the *known* through practice and visualization. Unsurprisingly, they won their competition against the group that didn't practice — and they did so easily.

No matter what unknown you face, you can prepare and practice for it. You can do research. You can visualize. You can do trial runs. If you're worried about getting to an interview on time, you go there the day before and try out the route while timing it. If you're worried about what you'll say in the interview, you study the company, read its website, read through its public newsletters, etc. If you're afraid of going bowling for the first time while on a date with someone new, you go out to that bowling alley the weekend before and try it out for yourself. No matter what it is, if you prepare ahead of time, you'll find your fear of the unknown evaporates.

It's like that old joke about the kid who's nervous for his test. He studies and studies and studies. When he gets done, he says, "I don't know what I was so worried about. That's the easiest test I ever took." The test was only easy because he was prepared, and that, of course, is the punch line.

FEAR OF FINANCIAL FAILURE

It's normal to fear financial failure. Everything we do or don't do in life revolves around money (which is why you're reading this book). You may not be making the money you want to make specifically because you're afraid of overextending your resources. There are a lot of pyramid schemes and other scams out there, too, that are designed to bilk you out of your money on the premise of making more. You know, selling knives door to door, or selling nutritional supplements, or any of several schemes that require you to pay out money before you start earning money.

That's a good rule of thumb, in fact: While it's normal to spend money to make money (for example, if you buy supplies to make crafts that you sell at a markup), any business that asks you first to *pay* for something before you start earning should be looked at very closely. It's not *necessarily* a scam... but you need to tread carefully.

Every opportunity you examine must be looked at this closely. Run the numbers. Do the math. Make sure that this way to make money actually benefits you (as well as your customers). You can run these numbers with any job you'll ever work, too. If you take a job that pays X, but your travel expenses to get to and from the job add up to X plus 1, it wouldn't make sense to take that job, would it? If you can make money selling painted widgets, but the price you get on eBay or Etsy for the widgets adds up to the cost of the widgets plus the cost of the paint, you didn't make a profit. All you did was find a self-sustaining hobby.

To overcome fear of financial failure, therefore, do the math before you embark on any venture. Make sure you know what the costs are and what the eventual profits will be. If you want to drive for Uber, for example, you need to know how much you can make versus how much your fuel will cost (and how to consider the mileage added on to your vehicle). Don't worry, though. You don't have to do all these computations yourself. There are plenty of people online who've already done the research. Just start searching and researching online. Take notes. Work out the costs... then test them out to make sure.

Once you've done your "due diligence," the fear of financial failure evaporates. It comes down to numbers, and accurate numbers don't lie.

FEAR OF REJECTION

Fear of rejection is a little more primal. We don't like putting ourselves out there only to fail. We don't like asking for something only to be refused. Many people fear selling because they fear being told "no." If your psyche simply can't stand up to being refused, then no, sales is not for you. The overwhelming majority of us, however, can learn to cope with rejection. It's just a matter of repetition.

You may have heard of "pick up artists." These are people who have specifically chosen to live a lifestyle of dating as much as possible. They take pride in how many women they've dated, and they have an entire lore built around how to get women to say "yes" to a date. The simplest principle of their lifestyle, however, is numbers: The more women you ask out, the higher the probability that, sooner or later, one of them says yes.

Well, the fear of rejection in sales can be overcome the same way. The *more* you sell, the more you'll *sell*. (This does, however, raise the question of how you'll know you've made the sale. We'll talk about that later on in the book.) Through repetition, you'll learn that rejection isn't a big deal. If you get rejected, you can be persistent or you can move on to the next prospect... but either way, you'll eventually sell to someone else. The more you practice, the better you'll get, and the less significant individual rejections will seem.

FEAR OF OVERWORK

Many of us are underemployed, or not making as much money as we could, because we value our free time. We don't want our lives to be nothing but work, work, work, and so we avoid opportunities through which we might make more money. We tell ourselves there's more to life than work (and there is). We rationalize our failure to achieve in any number of ways.

It doesn't have to work like that. You can make more money, yet not spend all your time working. You may have heard the old slogan, "Work smarter, not harder." Well, if you plan your sales, if you pick your money-making opportunities, in ways that don't require you to spend a lot of time on them, you can be making money right now with only a little effort up front.

For example, let's say you start making and selling craft items (something we'll discuss later in this book). That's something that involves a little up-front effort to create the crafts. Once those are made, however, the items sit on sales sites like Etsy and eBay and require very little intervention from you. The income rolls in every time your phone chimes to tell you a sale has been made. Your store front operates without your direct effort, twenty-four hours a day, and even around the world. That's one example of working smarter rather than harder.

Yes, you'll need to analyze how much extra effort is involved in every money-making opportunity. And yes, to make more money will require more work from you to earn it. The good news, though, and the reason you need not fear overwork, is that there are any number of ways to make money without working yourself to death for it.

FEAR OF MISTAKES

This is another primal fear that you can overcome with some simple psychology. We all fear making mistakes. We don't want to undertake a business venture only to have it fail. Stick with our example from before: Let's say you start selling crafts on Etsy. You make a bunch of your painted widgets, put them up for sale... and nobody buys them. There are lots of mistakes you might have made. Maybe the price is too high and the widget simply can't be profitable. Maybe your description isn't pulling in buyers. Maybe there simply is no consumer demand for the product. Maybe there's some other issue.

Well, you can dwell on mistakes, or you can learn from them. Thomas Edison famously said, "I have not failed. I've just found 10,000 ways that won't work." Use your mistakes to provide data for future ventures. Build on what you've learned. For example, if you learn what doesn't work for your sales listings, do some research on what does sell to see what you might need to do differently.

Email marketers do something called a "split test" where they prepare two different emails to sell the same product. Then they send out the emails to see which one "converts" more — which one gets more people to click and buy. The email that doesn't work as well could be seen as a mistake, as a failure. It isn't, though, because the marketer has just learned through "failure" what to avoid. Learning what *not* to do is as important as figuring out what you *should* do.

Don't fear your mistakes. Think of them as a means of gathering data for future attempts. As long as you never spend more money than you can afford to lose on a venture, you'll come out ahead when you get the variables nailed down.

FEAR OF CONFLICT

Few of us like conflict. You may not be making as much money as you could be because you worry that people in your life — family, a spouse, even your friends — won't be supportive. Arguments over money are some of the biggest challenges for marriages. Money, and our friends' or family members' opinions about how we're handling ours, can create all kinds of friction.

The only way to overcome this kind of potential conflict is to do your homework. If you have thoroughly researched each money-making prospect, it's much harder for friends or family to argue with you. In rare cases, there may be people in your life who remain negative and unsupportive, however. If that happens, you'll need to weigh whether you should cut these people out of your life to prevent them further holding your back. That's not easy, and it's not really the topic of this book... but it's something to consider.

In any case, don't let a fear of conflict hold you back. If you've done your due diligence, there should be nothing to argue about. If there still *is* an argument, well, you have challenges that run deeper than making money.

FEAR OF SOMETHING ELSE

Finally, there may be something else, something I can't predict or describe, that you fear. If you're afraid of selling and that fear doesn't fall into any of the previous categories, force yourself to sit down with a pad of paper and a pen or pencil. Figure out, on paper, what it is that you're afraid of. What's bothering you? What is that really makes you afraid?

Here's a simple method for doing that. Sit down with a pad and paper. Do it the old-fashioned way, in hardcopy. Eliminate distractions. Now, make a list of the things you DO NOT fear. Just write down whatever comes to mind.

Next, write down a list of the things you do fear. Once you have both lists, rank them. Of the things you don't fear, which do you feel MOST insecure about? Cross it off. What thing do you feel most insecure about after that? Cross it off. Repeat until you have just one thing left. That's a strength.

Rank the list of your fears in order. What do you fear least of the things you are afraid of? Cross it off. Then pick the thing you fear more than that, but less than the others. Cross it off, too. By the time you're done you'll have just one major, overriding fear.

Finally, compare your one overriding fear to your biggest strength. How do they compare? Are they even related to each other? Does your strength counteract your fear, or do you need to do some more work to address it?

Once you know what that thing is, you can go "forward, towards the danger." In other words, face your fear and in that way eliminate it. If you identify the source of your fear, you can do the homework, preparation, and corrective action to meet and surpass it. Because there is an endless amount of specific fears you could face, you'll need to think this through carefully... but the solution is really just a combination of what we've discussed to this point. Prepare for it, make it known if it's unknown, practice, and use just a little bit of courage to get you started.

THERE ARE NO SUCCESS STORIES IN THIS BOOK

About here is where I thought about inserting a list of success stories — the tales of people who've started from nothing and worked their way up to real material (and personal, even spiritual) gains. Everyone loves a good success story. Look at Will Smith's film, *The Pursuit of Happyness*. It's a brilliant telling of the story of Chris Gardner, who endured poverty and hardship and made something of himself simply because he refused to give up. What could help you better overcome your fears than that?

Well, as inspiring as stories like that are, they aren't *your* story. Deep down, I don't think people really take a story like that and decide that if it worked for Chris Gardner, or other people like him, it will work for the next person who tries. The only thing that's going to prove to you that you can succeed is if you get a taste of success.

A friend of mine is an Internet marketer. He has his own successful business, in which he sends email to the list he's built over the years, offering them various products and services. His list has gotten so big that he even makes money selling access to the list for advertisers. He described to me how fearful he was when he put together his first offer and mailed it out. Would people read the message? Would they buy the product? Would all his effort be wasted?

He had to overcome his initial fear and take that first step. Nobody could do it but him. It didn't matter that other people had succeeded in Internet marketing before. Until he took that leap, he was never going to get the taste of success that propelled him forward.

He explained to me that he sent his message and then went to bed. In the morning, he was amazed at the income that had come into his account. The key was, *it had all happened while he was asleep.* He was instantly hooked, he said, and that taste of success is what drove him to become one of the more successful marketers in his industry today.

Until you take that leap and get your own taste of the results, you may not feel like this is "real." I want you to understand that it is. Other people do it every day.

Will you be one of them today?

So, WHAT Should You Sell?

DECIDING *WHAT* TO SELL IS AS IMPORTANT AS deciding *how* to sell. Unfortunately, it isn't always obvious what you should be selling in order to make more money. The choice may be more obvious in some cases compared to others, but if you just don't have your head in the "sales" mode, you may not be sure how to start. That's okay! When presented with a challenge like this, it's always a good idea to start with the "Princess Bride" approach.

THE PRINCESS BRIDE APPROACH

The Princess Bride is a 1987 movie based on a 1973 novel of the same name. In it, our hero (who has recently returned from being mostly dead) consults with his friends about storming a castle in order to rescue his lady love. He's been out of circulation while mostly dead, so he asks his friends: What are our liabilities? What are our assets? He's trying to assess, in other words, what's working against them and what they have to work with. Looking at both assets and liabilities is the key to working through this type of challenge.

Liabilities

First, determine your liabilities. These are the things that might work against you or could present potential obstacles. They aren't necessarily reasons you can't embark on a given sales venture. They just represent things you'll need to look out for and take care of.

For example, one of your liabilities might be a lack of start-up money. If you want to invest some money in supplies to make and sell crafts, you have to get that money from somewhere. Finding a way to save or borrow the money is one liability to overcome for your craft project.

Another liability might be a lack of time. You might have a full-time job already and the fact that you have to spend your workdays there means you have only limited "free" time in which to engage in a money-making project to supplement your income. Figuring out how to manage your time or making the sacrifice to have less free time in order to devote those hours to your work project, are ways you could overcome this liability.

No matter what the venture, sit down and brainstorm as many potential obstacles (liabilities) as possible. That way, you can build into your plan ways to overcome these issues. The result will be a more successful venture.

Assets

This is, arguably, a lot more fun than thinking about your liabilities. Your assets are anything you can use and leverage toward your project. Start-up funds are assets. Office equipment that you already own can be assets. Craft supplies you already have are assets. Skills that you possess, or can learn, are assets. Assets are the tools, materials, and skills that you'll use toward your money-making ventures. Sometimes, sitting down and listing your assets can point you to money-making ventures you didn't know about and hadn't considered.

For example, a friend of mine found himself out of work for an extended period of time. When looking for a job didn't work, he decided he needed to switch careers. The question he then faced was, "What career do I pick?" He sat down and performed a "Princess Bride" analysis of his assets and liabilities.

One of his assets, he realized, was a state pistol permit. He lived in a state where handguns were heavily regulated, but he had taken the time to get a license to carry one. Using that license, he was able to apply for the credentials to become an armed security guard — something that was in demand and which pays much better than unarmed guard positions. He "sold" himself and his permit in order to get a new position in a field he had not previously considered.

You don't have to know what you'll use your assets to do when you first make your list. Make the list and then explore what you *might* do based on what you already have (or what you know you can get). A simple analysis of your assets and liabilities will often lead you down paths you didn't realize were options.

WHAT CAN YOU OFFER?

With your assets and liabilities in mind, then, ask yourself: "What can I offer?" Based on a complete list of your assets, for example, there may be things you can make. There may also be things you know how to do. Perhaps one of your assets is a strong back; you could do manual labor. Perhaps one of your assets is the knowledge of how to tie flies for fishing. You could start an online business selling your flies. You could also attend fishing events where your flies might also be sold. Maybe one of your assets is a car that meets Uber and Lyft's requirements; you could drive for one of these services in your free time.

Don't be afraid to think outside the box and consider unconventional ways to trade what you do, who you are, and what you know to make money. Maybe you are an expert in fitness and nutrition. You could offer your consulting services (assuming there is no licensing requirement for that). Then again, maybe there *is* a licensing requirement. That would be a liability you could potentially overcome by getting the credentials... and then your license becomes an asset that helps you make money.

It all comes down to what you can offer. What product can you make and sell? What product can you obtain in bulk and resell at a markup? What product can you modify and sell for more money? What skill do you have that you can sell? What knowledge do you have that you can offer for money? What manual labor are you willing to do in exchange for pay?

Don't worry about how to market what you do right now. We're not at that point yet (although we will be). Right now, just figure out what your options are. What do you offer to the marketplace?

WHAT CAN YOU OFFER MORE OF THAT YOU ALREADY DO?

I've included this as its own section because many people overlook it. You may be doing something right now that makes some money on the side. Because you're already doing that, you may not consider it when looking to make more money. That's a mistake. If you're already offering something for sale — some good, some service, etc. — you can always be offering MORE of it and making more money though an established sales channel.

There's Almost Always a Way to Grow

For example, maybe you make a couple of hundred dollars a year, or even a month, selling the occasional item on eBay. You may think, "Well, I only sell things when I have extra junk to get rid of. That's not an income stream." Why not? It certainly could be if you wanted it to be. For example, you could go to local thrift stores and find items that look unusual or which you think you can resell at a markup.

A local thrift store has only the customers that come through its doors. A site like eBay, by contrast, has thousands and thousands of customers all over the world. Buying something for one price at a thrift store and then relisting it as an online auction (with your purchase prices as the *starting* price) would be one way to break even and possibly make a healthy profit. I know a fellow who makes several hundred dollars a month just combing thrift stores for items to resell on auction sites.

Whatever you're doing right now that brings in income already, you should look at it carefully. Can it be scaled up? Can it be expanded? Can it bring in more funds than it already does, even if you have to find more inventory to sell... or more hours of your time to devote to it?

Determine Your Income Streams

With your assets, liabilities, and current selling activities in mind, choose something to offer and then run the numbers to see if you can make a profit at it. Based on what you have available (skills, materials, time, etc.), what can you offer? If you're not already selling it, what could it be?

SOME BASIC WAYS TO FIND NEW THINGS OR SERVICES TO SELL

Now, here's the thing: Maybe you engage in this whole process and you don't have something. Maybe you simply do not have a product or service in mind. Does that mean you can't make more money? Not at all! There are a few basic methods for finding new products or services to offer. These are the reconnaissance method, the coattails method, and the services method. Any or all of them can point you to ways to make money.

The Reconnaissance Method

One way to find new goods and services to sell is to look at what's *already* selling. You might be able to sell it, too. Remember fidget spinners? Briefly, they were very popular. They started out in just a few stores, but when everybody wanted to buy one, they started popping up at the checkouts in grocery stores, drug stores, and just about everywhere else. Sellers on eBay and Etsy started offering them too and, if they were fast enough to cash in on the fad, they did pretty well for themselves.

Whenever you can identify a popular product, chances are good that you can sell some of that product too (especially if you offer it at a lower price, or with better customer service, or with faster shipping, or just in a different venue. When a product is popular, there is room for everyone (at least until the market gets totally saturated).

You don't have to offer the identical product, either. Sometimes, offering something that is similar is enough to generate some sales. For example, at the time of writing this book, elaborate beaded necklaces are very popular in certain circles. Buddhist style necklaces with skulls and other heavy beads seem to be selling well to the male jewelry-and-pocketknife market. Anyone can make beaded necklaces if they're willing to buy the materials and put in the time. You could cash in on that trend and sell a similar product that appeals to the same market.

One way to find out what's popular is simply to look at what's already selling. Look at the craft sites. Look at the auction sites. What terms autocomplete, indicating what people search for often? What product listings do you see over and over again? What's featured? Look at the prices that things are going for.

Look at the items flagged as bestsellers. With a little research in any of these online marketplaces, you can learn a lot about what products are popular... and then you can cash in on the trend.

The Coattails Method

Related to the reconnaissance method is the coattails method. This means you find a popular product... and then you sell something that goes with that product or is inspired by it. I can think of a couple of good examples from my own friends and acquaintances to illustrate this concept.

One fellow I know makes knife sheaths out of a plastic material called Kydex and sells them online. He tried a few different models, but none were selling well. Then a specific type of paring knife became very popular because it was endorsed by a couple of figures in the market — self-defense instructors who recommended that knife. My friend started offering a version of his plastic sheaths for these knives... and they became his single most popular item.

A friend-of-a-friend identified a certain toy, a kind of stuffed animal, that was very popular on the market. The toy has a little bed that is hard to get. This ingenious fellow found a pet bed that was about the same size, bought them in bulk, and started listing them on auction sites as the perfect bed for the stuffed animal. He sold quite a few of them by "riding the coattails" of this popular product.

If you can identify what's already selling and what's popular, you might be able to find a way to market to the buyers of that product by selling them things that go with the product (or things that are similar to and related to the product). Again, most of what you need to know is right on the auction sites and craft sites waiting to be identified. You just have to spend some time searching through it to see what people want (and how much they're paying to get it).

The Services Method

Finally, you could offer a service. There are any number of services you could offer, and any number of skills you could learn. But how do you know what to offer? Again, do your homework online to see what people ALREADY are searching for. Do searches to see what autocompletes in Google for terms like "wanted" and "wanted to hire." See what people are looking for. You might be surprised how easy it is to make some money.

For example, it's incredibly hard to find reliable snow shoveling. I don't know why but hiring a service to plow and shovel your driveway is kind of a crapshoot. Every season you hear about plow services who never show up. Finding someone who'll just shovel out a driveway manually, including your steps and walkway, is even harder.

Knowing this, you could list your services online through an app, on Craigslist, on social media, and so on. All you need is a strong back, a snow shovel, and willingness to get up early on snowy days. If you have the time, the will, and the muscle, you could make quite a bit of money doing this... all by identifying that people are ALWAYS looking for plowing and shoveling services in the winter.

Social media can be very helpful because many sites, like Facebook, include local groups and online marketplaces where people post about what they need. Don't just look for what people want to hire, though. Look at what is being offered. There is room for more than one person doing the same thing in the same market. You'll get ideas and you may also be able to compete on price (not to mention quality of service).

A FEW VENUES TO CHECK OUT

I'm going to be honest with you: There are way more websites for this type of thing than I can possibly list here. There are freelance sites like Upwork, where you can set up a profile and then bid on jobs that range from editing to writing to graphic design (and more). There are sites and apps like Takl and TaskRabbit that let you trade your labor for cash. There are other sites and apps like Fiverr, Etsy, and eBay where you can sell, resell, and even offer a variety of skills and services. The market is always changing and the sites that are most popular change as time goes on. What you need to do, therefore, is search the Web for whatever sites are current.

Check them out and then search for the names of those apps specifically. Look at their ratings in your app store. Check for user experiences online. Etsy is known for crafts, but people sell just about anything you can imagine there. By contrast, eBay is known as an auction site, but you can set up an entire online storefront there. You can do the same on Facebook. Some websites and apps, like Shopify, offer drop-ship reselling, allowing you to set up an entire website and then sell products without ever actually handling the inventory itself.

Do your homework and determine the venues that are best for you. Don't be afraid to try more than one. For example, you may find that you do more sales on Etsy, but not nearly as many on eBay. Or the reverse might be true. You may be surprised by the results, too, because what you THINK might sell best on a given platform doesn't. Sometimes, the results defy your best attempts to predict them. Don't worry about that.

Test out multiple sites to determine where you should concentrate your efforts (unless you have no trouble keeping up with all of them). If there are listing fees involved, this will factor into your decisions. (Don't forget to include those fees in your liabilities!)

How to Sell

ALL RIGHT. YOU HAVE IDENTIFIED THE FACT THAT, in order to make more money, you need to start selling. Whether you're selling yourself in the form of your services, selling yourself in the form of a job application, or selling goods or services to customers, you know that you do need to sell. You've embraced and defined what you're going to sell. What does that leave?

It leaves the how. *How* will you sell? Too many people think of sales as going door to door, desperate to convince (or simply con) people into giving them money. *This is not sales.* Never think of selling as inflicting yourself on other people, or as imposing your will on them. Grabbing someone by the lapels and telling them how lucky they are to have your product or service won't do anything but drive customers away.

That brings us to the question of how to sell. There are a few different components to it. We'll talk about a couple of introductory concepts before we introduce you to the Now Not Later sales system. It's not complicated and it's not hard. It's basically just a few step-by-step pieces of advice. Anyone can follow it and anyone can use it to make more money right away.

PEOPLE DON'T BUY PRODUCTS OR SERVICES; THEY BUY YOU

One of the most fundamental principles of sales is that people aren't really buying what you're selling. They're not truly looking at your product, your service, or your resume. Sure, those are factors. On a surface or intellectual level, they are looking at those things. To be honest, though, if they didn't think you could help them, potentially (your product is something that interests them, your service is something they need, your skills meet their criteria and thus you got the interview, etc.), they wouldn't be listening.

Most people dismiss out of hand anything that doesn't interest them or which they simply cannot afford. If they're listening, they're already hooked on the basis of the product or service. It's YOU that makes or loses the sale. That's why one of the basic facts of sales is that people don't buy what you're selling. They buy YOU as a person.

The key to making sales, then, is to be genuine. People love truth. They love honesty. They love people whom they see as dealing with them "straight," as not shining them on or trying to trick them. Chances are good that when I say the phrase, "used car salesman," your reaction is negative. You think of people trying to push things on you and trick you into buying, don't you? That's common... and it's the result of that "always be closing" approach to bullying people into buying. It doesn't work and it never really has; it's simply given "sales" a bad name.

What if I told you that a man with almost no personality, no looks, no political experience, and no prayer of winning once changed the course of a political election? His name was Ross Perot, and when he ran for president against George W. Bush and challenger Bill Clinton, he had no prayer of winning. All he had working for him was the perception that he was *honest* — that he, as an outsider with no political experience, had no reason to lie.

Based on that genuine approach to politics, Perot won 19 percent of the popular vote. It wasn't enough to win, but it was a HUGE percentage for someone nobody had ever heard of before... and it was enough to deny Bush reelection and change the course of history. He did all of that simply by being genuine... and for a lot of voters, that was enough.

Being yourself, being authentic, will be the key to every sale you make. When you build relationships with those to whom you sell, when you get to know them as a human being, when you treat them honestly and they perceive that earnestness in you, they'll be inclined to give you their business.

Does the Value Outweigh the Investment?

Authenticity and trust are incredibly important. The other component is the value exchanged. Everyone asks themselves if the price they are giving for a good or service (or to compensate an employee) is outweighed by what they'll get. You would be surprised, however, how much who you are as a person factors into that equation.

Think about it: You have the choice of two repair shops for your car. One has much lower prices, but you don't know anything about it. The other has a proven history of dealing with you honestly and saving you money by not charging you for repairs you don't need. Are you going to take your car to the new, cheaper place, or keep taking it to the honest shop you can trust?

The only way to build that perception of trust, and thus to have that trust factored in as a value in the "investment" question your customers ask themselves, is to be authentic. Honesty sells. Be who you are and make sure you deal openly and honestly with everyone. It will pay off. You will sell, and you will make more money... right now.

Selling Begins with Listening

It's not enough just to be yourself, of course. You actually have to engage in the process of selling (and we'll get to our specific process for that). That process STARTS with listening.

Listening is all about finding what people believe that they want and need. You'll be an active participant in this process. Listening, remember, is not just staying quiet and waiting to talk. It is actively gathering information from the person who is telling you what they desire. People buy because they perceive they have a want, need, or challenge/problem to solve.

Listening and asking questions is NOT interrogating people. You'll develop your relationship with them by being authentically you — by being someone they can trust — even if your "relationship" is five minutes long and started when you introduced yourself for a job interview.

We Are All Selling, All the Time

If what I've told you up to this point seems simple, even *too* simple, there's a reason for that: It IS simple. The fact is, most books on sales are way too complicated. They expect you to memorize techniques, methods, and even memorized lines that you're never going to use in real life. Or rather, if you do use it in real life, you will sound fake and forced. In other words, you'll sound the opposite of authentic, genuine, and honest... and because of that, you won't make sales.

You've got to let go of the notion that selling is about manipulating people or *making* them buy. It's not. Selling is something you do FOR someone. You present them with an opportunity that they WANT to take.

When you focus on being authentic and honest, building genuine relationships with people, and presenting them with a value that outweighs the cost of what they've got to pay to get it... they're going to buy. They're going to buy you first and the value second, but they're going to buy regardless. That leads me to the Now Not Later sales system.

WHY LISTENING MATTERS

You can learn a lot about what people should be doing, when it comes to sales, by looking at what they are doing *wrong*. I spent decades working with other professionals, for whom sales was part of the job (just like it is for everyone). Too often, they started their presentations by telling prospective clients everything they knew about whatever it was they thought the prospect wanted to buy. They thought if they just *told* the prospect all about the options, instead of asking the prospect what he or she wants and needs, they can muscle the sale through this adult show-and-tell display.

That doesn't work. You can't swamp the client in information and hope to get a positive response. You've GOT to listen. Otherwise, you'll make assumptions about other people's needs based on what YOU think, not on what THEY think.

A superior sales methodology is to ask questions to find out the person's true needs, desires, challenges, and business and personal goals. I call these "need development" questions.

Assume the role of a consultant and then recommend to them the type of solution that best satisfies their needs.

It's an axiom that people don't care how much you know until they know how much you care. Flooding a person with information about how well you know your area of expertise only makes them shut down mentally and classify you as someone who only wants to sell them something. The only reason why anyone ever buys anything is because they perceive they have a need, an unfulfilled desire, or an unsolved challenge or problem.

You should be asking open-ended questions (and don't worry, we'll get to the actual sales system in a little bit). Open-ended questions begin with the words "who, what, when, where, how, or why".

People want to be listened to and they want to be understood. When you listen to them and let them know that you understand what they have told you, you are paying them one of the highest compliments you can give to another person. At the same time, you are developing a firm understanding of their needs. Only after you have a comprehensive, as possible, understanding of the prospect's real needs and "big picture" have you earned the right to talk about your products and solutions.

Another benefit of asking the right questions and taking a consultative approach is that it increases the level of trust the prospect has for you and it allows the prospect to feel like they are "buying" rather than feeling like you are "selling". The fact is, people are more likely to buy from you if they think it is their idea rather than your idea. They recognize you care. They recognize you want to make the mental transition to their side of the desk. They perceive you as a partner and not a vendor. Instead of you selling them…they buy from you.

People quickly recognize when you are trying to sell them something — or, even worse, *manipulate* them into buying. And while some people may submit to this approach or manipulative tactics because they have an overwhelming need, many more people will tell you, "I want to think it over." Or, "we'll get back to you after we think it over." They put you in the category of commodity and once they perceive you as the same as everyone else, the decision becomes price and delivery focused. The end result is lost confidence, lost credibility and lost sales.

When you meet with someone, whether in-person or online, odds are they are very busy, and they may have you pegged as a sales type who is going to try and sell whatever it is you have to offer. Very seldom do they meet someone who is focused on <u>their</u> needs, wants, challenges, and expectations. Even more seldom do they meet someone who asks the kinds of questions that add value to the meeting. Questions they haven't even thought of before.

Separate yourself from all the other people who have interacted with them in the past. Discover their real needs and desires. Then, let them know you understand them by repeating back to them what they've told you.

Remember, people only buy to fill their own needs -- not yours. It's a lot easier (and a lot more profitable) to listen people into buying than it is to try to talk them into buying.

THE NOW NOT LATER SALES SYSTEM

Everyone who says they're teaching you about selling will have some kind of system. Most are too complicated. This one is very simple. It's something anyone can learn and, to be honest, it's mostly common sense. As the old saying goes, the conundrum with common sense is that it isn't very common. Our system has just five steps: Prepare, Create the Questions You Need to Ask, Ask the Questions, Shut up (shut up, shut up), and How to Know When You've Made the Sale.

1. Prepare

You may be tempted to think, once you have some experience under your belt, that you don't have to prepare for each and every attempt to sell. That's not true. You have to prepare EVERY time. Always do some homework on who you're trying to sell to. If you're about to post a new sales listing on your Etsy page, you need to research that. If you're about to sit for a job interview, you must research the company (and preferably the person you're interviewing with). If you're going to talk to someone about an investment opportunity, you have to research your prospect. Every single time you try to make a sale, you have to do your homework. Don't skimp and don't take shortcuts. Every time you fail to prepare, you prepare to fail.

2. Create the Questions You Need To Ask

We've said that selling starts with listening. Well, you need to direct that listening toward something productive. Have you heard of the Six Honest Serving Men? The Six Honest Serving Men were memorialized by Rudyard Kipling. Part of a longer poem, these lines comprise part of the epigraph to Kipling's short story, "The Elephant's Child." They go like this:

I keep six honest serving-men
(They taught me all I knew);
Their names are What and Why and When
And How and Where and Who.

It's that simple. You need to know the what, the why, the when, the how, the where, and the who. The specific nature of those questions depends on the opportunity. For example, say you're selling yourself for a job. What is the job? Why are you the best candidate for the job? When will you be needed to start? How will you do the job? Where will the job take place? Who will you be working with? Those are just some of the questions you should be supplying answers to, and which you'll need answered by the employer (depending on the context). The "six honest serving men" apply differently according to every situation, but if you ask those questions, you WILL get the information you want.

During the preparation phase, it should become obvious in which ways to ask these questions. Figure that out before you start, not on the fly. Use the Six Honest Serving Men as a guide to setting up the questions you'll need answered... or that you'll have to answer as part of the sales process.

3. Ask the Questions

This may seem obvious, but it's a formal step in the process for a very specific reason. I once interviewed a sales professional who explained that he'd gotten a job, as a young man, because he was the only person who "asked for the sale." It isn't enough to know what questions to ask. You've got to make sure you ask them. Don't be afraid to "ask for the sale" as part of your questions. It's up to the prospect to answer you. Your job is to guide them as they provide the information you need. That's where listening comes in. You ask your questions, and then... well, refer to the next step.

4. Shut Up, Shut Up, Shut Up

When someone is answering your questions, don't interrupt. Listen and write down the answers. Make it clear you are making notes. Maintain regular eye contact and jot down what you're learning so that you don't have to ask twice. Your prospect's time should be treated with respect. It's valuable, and the person to whom you are listening will appreciate that you treat him or her that way.

Here's a story I can tell you along those lines. In 1971, after working as a photojournalist, I decided to open a studio-based photography business. I was very young and was under the impression that if I built a really great studio along with creating and presenting great work, the public would be knocking down my door. It didn't work like that.

I quickly realized that people were not ready to listen to what I had to say about my photography. It was only after I realized I had to get their attention first that I began to experience success.

As I got more experience in marketing and sales, this is what I learned: In order to get people to listen to what I had to say and buy what I had to sell, I had to listen to them first. I learned the value of asking questions and listening before trying to sell or market. I realized that attempting to sell something without listening to my customers first would be the same thing as a physician prescribing a drug without ever talking to the patient. I would be guilty of malpractice.

Listen with Your Eyes and Heart

Let's say you're at a party and it's a good networking opportunity. How long do you think the average person takes to make a decision about someone they've just met? How long does it take for your gut to say, "I like this person?" or "Wow, get me out of here!" If you're like most people you'll have that gut feeling within the first few minutes—sometimes less.

How do you come to a decision about someone else? Is it their dress, the tone or volume of their voice, the words they use, mannerisms, their smile, eye contact (or lack thereof)? Do they look around the room as you're being introduced, or do they make you feel like they're truly interested in you?

All of these things are part of the way we make a first impression. There are several ways you can take advantage of this. For one thing, learn how to match someone's tone and pace of speech. If you are caffeine-fueled, bouncing on the balls of your feet and speaking at warp speed, you're not going to connect with a calm, contemplative person who really thinks about each sentence. (In fact, they may well hate you.) Learn to use positive psychological reciprocity: Respond to another's positive action with one of your own. If your new acquaintance smiles, smile back. Watch them to keep it going.

There is a potential complication in our modern age, however: So much of our interactions with people take place through text. We never see or even hear these people. So how do you listen to someone you can't hear, or stay open and attentive with someone you can't see? Well, if modern video teleconferencing (like Skype or the many other platforms available for this) is an option, you can do that. A lot of the time, however, you'll be interacting with people through text exclusively.

Practice communicating with people through text. Be friendly, ask questions, listen to the answers, and pay close attention to the clues your text-based interactions give you. People usually reveal more than they think they are revealing — from the words they choose, to how they abbreviate, to how quickly they respond to text interactions.

It will take time, but you can learn to "read" what you're *reading*. You'll also learn, through practice, to respond in ways that the other party finds genuine and helpful. There are always ways to engender good will and trust, no matter what the medium. People do business with others they like and trust. Nurture a relationship with a client or potential client just like you would with someone you want to date.

5. When is it Time to Start Talking?

Once you've asked the questions that encourage the other person to tell you what they need, you've eventually got to explain why what you offer (yourself, your goods, your service, etc.) meets those needs.

It all hinges on value. Ask yourself how you can provide value to the other person. Focus on providing value and the rest will fall into place. But sooner or later, it is indeed your turn to talk after you've listened to the other person.

Many years ago, a wise man suggested I picture a balance scale, like the Scale of Justice. It has two sides. You have to put enough value on one side of the scale to outweigh the investment the other person will make. As we've already said, the value must outweigh the cost. By asking questions to determine the person's needs, wants, desires, requirements, you get the information you need to keep going. Then, you ask development questions to determine if you can satisfy the other person's needs. As the conversation progresses, you explain how you'll do that for them.

It's best to use real-life examples and stories. In an interview or a sales pitch, that's obvious. In a sale's listing online, that could take the form of customer testimonials, or even just you telling stories as part of the listing. There's something else you must consider, though, and that's the truth.

Don't be Afraid of the Truth

What you're selling may not be the answer. The answer might be to find a better solution. You might not be the right person for the job. Your product might not satisfy the potential customer's needs. Every single circumstance is different.

People will always have objections, of course, even when what you're selling perfectly meets their needs. If you have addressed any objections and negotiated all necessary components, THEN you know you've made the sale. Closing is simply a matter of asking for the sale — of asking them to take whatever action is necessary for the deal to be sealed. It's not a trick and it's nothing manipulative. You don't "close" until you know you've sold, and you don't know you've sold until you've addressed their objections, negotiated the solutions, and determined that your value meets their needs.

HOW TO KNOW WHEN YOU'VE
MADE THE SALE

I've basically just told you how to know when you've made the sale, but I want to add that it's definitely not "ABC" – Always Be Closing. Salespeople love to quote Alec Baldwin's obnoxious character in Glengarry Glen Ross. The way the salespeople in that movie operate is definitely not what you want to be. Tricking people, deceiving them, and manipulating them is what people tend to THINK sales are. They picture a character like Baldwin's forcing sales by being incredibly aggressive... essentially, bullying people into spending their money. It doesn't work that way.

Customers, employers, and prospects know the challenges they face much better than you do. Don't make the mistake of thinking that you already have the solutions. To assume you know the solution before you really understand the challenges, once again, is like a physician writing a prescription before making a diagnosis.

Likewise, remember that positive customer relationships are not just about getting paid. The prospect might not need what you're selling — this time. But if you do know how to solve their problems and challenges (even if it doesn't mean a sale for you) don't you owe it to them to provide that solution? Would you rather be thought of as the salesperson who sells (insert anything here) or as the person who provides value regardless of your reward? Helping people only when you are getting paid falls short of best sales practices — and best life practices.

After the Sale
You should be sending your customers signs of your appreciation — a thank you note, a gift, flowers — after every sale. After an interview, you send a letter. After a sale online, you send a thank-you email. After a meeting with an important potential client, you send flowers or snacks. It's very simple, but few people ever actually do it. Here's the key: You need to do it *immediately*. It should be sent the same day, or the following day at the latest.

Why? Well, there's the obvious need to say thank you. Just as important, though, is to reassure the other person that they made the correct decision. Salespeople have a saying: It isn't really a sale until the check cashes. This will help get that check through the bank. It takes away buyer's remorse. Even if the "check" is metaphorical and not literal, it's the same thing.

Possibilities

NOW THAT YOU'VE READ THE THEORY, IT'S TIME
to consider some examples. Most people learn better when they
have some examples to use as models. That's normal. What you
have to remember, when reading through this list of examples,
is that these are just the BEGINNING of the possibilities. You
can apply the principles in this book to just about any possibility.
All you have to do is follow the instructions already on these
pages. In the next section, you'll find a list of action steps that
outlines how the process works.

Okay, here are just a few examples:

SELLING SOMETHING YOU MAKE

The first and most obvious way to make money is to create some kind of craft item and sell it for money. For example, let's say you have artistic talent and you create art prints for sale.

How To Apply The System

First, identify what kind of art prints you think people want. You may stumble into a fad or trend (or many of them). You may also be able to do some research on or in the sales venue.

Next (and this may be part of the first step), identify the sales venue. Will you be selling online at eBay or Etsy? Will you be buying table or booth space at local craft fairs and events? Identify all the costs associated with these. Call around, search online, contact the venues (or search their FAQ files online), and keep detailed notes.

Third, identify all your costs. Once you have identified the costs, set the price for your art prints at a level that allows you as much profit as you think the market will bear. Compare your prices to those for similar art prints. You'll need to be competitive unless you want to be undercut by other sellers.

Fourth, do some test sales. Set up a few listings online or buy space at a single craft fair. See if your idea can make a profit, at least potentially. Treat the initial sales as an opportunity to do some market research, too.

Finally, evaluate your success. How did you do? Can you see yourself making a profit at this, or is it better to move on to the next idea? How can you reduce costs and make more profit, or increase sales to do the same? The evaluation step is extremely important.

SELLING SOMETHING YOU DON'T MAKE

The next and similarly obvious way to make money is to buy something you don't make and resell it at a profit. The steps are exactly the same as selling something you do make. The only difference is that you know your costs because you know the unit cost for the item you're buying.

How To Apply The System

For example, during the "fidget spinner" craze, you could be buying fidget spinners from a supplier and reselling them. Take the time to get a distributor account and/or a reseller's license in order to get the lowest price for the fidget spinners (or whatever you're selling). Buying in bulk saves money, but if you buy too much inventory and it doesn't sell, you could end up stuck with a loss. That's why the small tests to start out are so important.

PROVIDING A SERVICE IN PERSON

What can you do? What are you good at? What are you WILLING to do? Let's say you decide to mow lawns to make money. This might seem quite simple, but you'll still need to apply the system.

How To Apply The System

You'll need to factor the cost of gasoline for your mower, maintenance for your mower, and transportation for you and your mower to the locations you'll serve. You'll also need to identify a way to reach your customers. Perhaps you'll ask around the neighborhood (where your listening skills come into play immediately). Perhaps you'll list yourself with one of the many service apps. There are snow shoveling and lawn mowing apps, for example, that let you set up a profile and then accept jobs that are pitched to the marketplace.

After you've performed the service a few times, you'll need to evaluate your profit again. After you subtract the fuel costs, transportation costs, time involved, etc., are you making enough money to call it a profit? Can you raise your prices? Should you lower them and, if you do, what will your profit be then? Analyzing your progress on an ongoing basis is critical to making this work.

PROVIDING A SERVICE ONLINE

The online marketplace offers up a host of possibilities. For example, let's say you have skill as an editor. You could offer your skill editing other people's work online through a multitude of different freelancer marketplaces.

How To Apply The System

First, pick a venue (or multiple venues), like Fiverr and Upwork. Now, set up your profile. List your editing job. You'll need to determine how much editing you'll offer, how many editing passes are part of the service, how much you're charging for that quantity of editing, and what you'll do if a customer is unhappy.

After you've done some editing jobs, your math will center on how much money you made versus how much time and effort was spent. Is the exchange worth your time? Are you happy with the "profit margin" where the "sweat of your brain" is concerned?

YOUR OWN IDEA

By now, you're seeing the basic and broad strokes for applying the system to any idea of your own. It's honestly that simple. The only thing complicated about it has been trying to mention all of the possibilities in these pages — which is quite impossible. That's why we take a principle-based approach and apply the system to whatever specific scenario you can imagine.

How To Apply The System

There's a checklist in the next section, but basically, you identify the good or service, you identify the audience, you listen to the audience, and then you set your pricing based on your costs. Once you've got all that in place, you perform some test sales and evaluate the results.

Now, Not Later: Your Action Checklist

FOR EVERY SINGLE IDEA YOU HAVE, EVERY SALES opportunity, every money-making chance that comes along, do the following. This list is a generalized set of action steps for applying the Now, Not Later sales system. Adapt the ten steps to your specific idea and you'll be positioned for the best possible chance at success.

1. Define your idea.
2. Define your [potential] audience.
3. What does your audience want, need, and think about the potential idea?

4. What do you know about your idea? Identify the gaps, then fill them.

5. What are ALL the costs associated with your idea (creating the good or service to be sold and making it available for sale)?

6. What are ALL the costs associated with fulfilling your idea (getting the good or service to the buyer).

7. Communicate with your audience to better identify and define the need to be filled.

8. Sell to your audience. Are there additional costs associated with this step (advertising, listing fees, etc.)?

9. Provide after-sales support to your audience. How can you make your customers REPEAT customers?

10. Assess your profitability. What did you make after costs, and how much of your time was involved? How much are you making per hour? Can anything be changed? Should it be changed? Does the idea remain viable?

If you follow these ten steps with every idea, adapting and making the list more specific as you go, you'll find further ways to refine your action steps. Don't be afraid to buy a notebook and keep detailed notes and/or back up data files on your computer, tablet, or phone.

Knowledge is power. Data is money. Keep detailed notes and refer back to the information you amass. You'll be amazed at how it can help you.

Get Started NOW, Not Later

THIS BOOK IS NOT LONG BECAUSE YOUR TIME IS valuable. This book is not complicated because making money is not difficult. This book explains that there is money just waiting to be earned... and that you need only apply the basic steps of the Now, Not Later sales system to start putting that money in your pocket.

But I can hear you asking yourself: "If it's that simple, why isn't everybody doing it?"

Well, that's another fact of human nature. People don't do things because they THINK the effort involved will be too much. They THINK the task is too hard. They THINK it's easier to want money, to complain about money, to worry about money... yet so few of them ever actually get up off their behinds and MAKE money.

Well, you're reading this book because you're ready to do just that. You now have in your hands a simple set of blueprints for making money out of just about any idea you might have. The limits are, literally, what you can imagine. That's a cliché, certainly, but it's also true.

What can you imagine? Okay, now apply the system: What will it cost? What does your audience want? Where do you find them? How can you listen to them? Once you've done that, ask yourself: How did I do... and should I keep doing it?

It's that simple, but if you never start, you won't make a dime.

Make that money. Make it NOW, not later.

You'll be glad you did.

Thank you for taking the time to read this book. It was written to help you in the spirit with which others have helped us. If you need anything, or if there's any other information or help we can provide, please reach out to us at the Poole Consulting Group website,

https://bobpoole.com.